CREATIVE

PHOTOGRAPHY

Linda Wevill

Matador
9 Priory Business Park,
Wistow Road, Kibworth Beauchamp,
Leicestershire, LE8 0RX
Tel: 0116 279 2299
Email: books@troubador.co.uk
Web: www.troubador.co.uk/matador
Twitter: @matadorbooks

ISBN 978 1838590 543
British Library Cataloguing in Publication Data.
A catalogue record for this book is available from the British Library.

Printed and bound in Malta by Gutenberg Press Ltd
Typeset in 11pt Lato by Troubador Publishing Ltd, Leicester, UK

Matador is an imprint of Troubador Publishing Ltd

For my husband Richard, my daughters Emma, Carla, and Amy,
and my grandchildren Max, Arlo, Luca and Cleo

CONTENTS

ACKNOWLEDGEMENT

I would like to thank my many photography friends for helping and inspiring me on my creative journey. Special thanks go to Mike Longhurst ARPS, for kindly agreeing to proof-read and comment on the book. When Mike did not understand what I had written, I knew I had not explained it properly. I am grateful to him for undertaking the task.

ABOUT THE AUTHOR

Linda Wevill is a creative photographer specialising in the landscape, although she enjoys capturing a diverse range of images from still life to travel. She is a Fellow of the Royal Photographic Society and serves on the RPS Assessment Panels.

Linda has exhibited widely both within the UK and internationally, including at the Royal Albert Hall, the National Theatre and the OXO Gallery in London and at the Huangshan Yixian International Festival in China. She has had her images and articles published in numerous photographic magazines and other publications. Linda is in demand as a speaker around the country and has run creative workshops for both the RPS and camera clubs.

Linda achieves a soft painterly effect in her photography and always aims to portray the essence of a place. She enjoys experimenting with techniques whether in-camera or during processing by, for example, varying shutter speeds at the time of shooting or using texture layers in Photoshop. Her aim is to express a personal depiction of her environment, to capture the atmosphere of the scene and the vision she is trying to convey.

'Creative Photography' is Linda's first book and it gives her great pleasure to be able to pass on tips and ideas gained through her experience over many years. Linda hopes the book will give readers the motivation to go out and experiment, using the techniques discussed, to move their photography forward and create their own style.

All the images in this book are Linda's and to see more of her work, please visit her website: www.lindawevillphotography.com or follow her on Facebook.

The images above are a selection from Linda's Royal Photographic Society Fellowship panel.

INTRODUCTION

An understanding of the basics of photography is obviously important, but only the starting point if you want your images to stand out from the crowd. To take different, more exciting images, a creative interpretation is required of the photographer. Creativity is about expressing your vision and emotions and portraying your subject in a way that is unique and exciting. The aim of this book is to share with you some ideas to move your photography forward by giving you the knowledge to experiment and explore the possibilities to create your own personal style.

Current trends in creative photography are looked at with advice and tips on the methods involved. In-camera techniques used for creating soft, painterly images, including experimenting with long shutter speeds, multiple exposures and intentional camera movement (ICM), are examined. Creative Photoshop techniques are also explained and the key to being able to work in this way is to master layer masks. They are essential for composite images to give a seamless blending of two or more images. How to work with layers and layer masks are explained in detail with screenshots to help your understanding. When experimenting with Photoshop the boundaries to your imagination are your only obstacles to creating truly original images.

Whether you are just starting out on your photographic journey or are an experienced photographer, this book will prove invaluable in giving you the skills and consequently the motivation to try something new. In the process you will discover more possibilities for creative work in any particular scene. The more you try out different techniques, and the more skilled you become, the more you will find yourself exploring new avenues, and your creative style will come through.

When experimenting the results are not always certain and exploration of a technique can often take on a life of its own. This can result in failure, but also achieve a result that surpasses your expectations. You should always remember to have fun and enjoy the process. That is what it should all be about!

'The real voyage of discovery consists not in seeking new landscapes, but in having new eyes.'

Quote by Marcel Proust

IN-CAMERA CREATIVE TECHNIQUES

Some photographers prefer to finalise their final images in-camera so they don't have to spend hours post-processing on their computer afterwards. The satisfaction here is in getting it right before the shutter is pressed.

We shall start by going through techniques that enable the photographer to produce creative images in-camera, starting with capturing movement with long exposures, intentional camera movement (ICM), going on to look at multiple exposures and finally considering other creative possibilities such as using different lenses and searching for more unusual shots, such as reflections, looking through glass and even abstract shapes and exploring colours in, for example, rust and ice patterns. All with the aim of encouraging the photographer to experiment and to look more closely at the world around them.

LONG EXPOSURES

Long exposures can give a surreal effect, moving away from reality, giving images a sense of mystery. They usually involve a long shutter speed to capture the stationary elements of images sharply, while blurring or obscuring the moving elements. We shall be looking at capturing the motion of the sea, movement in the landscape, such as leaves blowing in the wind, people on the move or any moving subject, fireworks, traffic trails and so on. The required shutter speed depends on the lighting conditions at the time and the effect you are trying to achieve. This is best explained with examples.

In this image you can see the slight movement of leaves moving in the breeze and also some movement of their reflection in the water, giving the scene a painterly quality.

Image 1 – Blowing Autumn Leaves

INTERPLAY BETWEEN THREE ELEMENTS OF EXPOSURE

When taking your camera off automatic mode, an understanding of the three elements of exposure is required; aperture, shutter speed and ISO. Understanding the interplay between these three elements will enable you to have control over your photography.

Aperture is the hole within a lens through which light travels into the camera body. The larger the aperture, the more light passes to the camera sensor. It determines an image's depth of field, which means how much of the image is in focus. A large depth of field (high Av number) will have sharp focus from foreground to background, while a shallow depth of field (small Av number) focuses on one particular plane, with the foreground and background elements being blurred.

Shutter speed is the length of time a camera shutter is open to expose light into the camera sensor. It controls how motion is captured by the camera, and we shall be going into this in great detail in our quest for more imaginative images. The slower the shutter speed, the longer the exposure time and more light reaches the sensor.

ISO is the 'film speed' carried over from the days of film, but means the same thing in digital terms i.e. sensitivity to light. A high ISO makes the sensor more sensitive to light, whereas a low ISO is less sensitive to light. In order not to lose quality you will want to keep your ISO setting as low as possible. Noise is the main problem with higher ISO levels, although with modern digital cameras the ISO setting can be greatly increased with little loss of quality.

A change to one of the elements of exposure will affect the other two. This is usually a compromise and your choice of settings will be dependent on what you are trying to achieve and which element is most important to you in your shot. A longer shutter speed will require a lower ISO or larger aperture size to maintain the same exposure value. That is, to ensure that the same amount of light hits the sensor.

There may, however, be circumstances when it will not be possible to compromise further and still have a correct exposure. For instance, if you want sharpness in crucial areas, like rocks, but softness in others, such as the sea, you will need to slow down your shutter speed to capture this movement. But this may prevent you from achieving correct exposure as too much light may now be hitting the sensor. If you are shooting early or late in the day when light levels are low, your shutter speeds will already be slow so, in these circumstances, you have more flexibility. But they may still not be slow enough to achieve the amount of motion capture you desire with the correct exposure. This is where Neutral Density filters may be necessary to give you complete control and capture the shot you envisage.

This image shows the effects of a 5 second shutter speed. The movement of the water over the rock in the foreground is smooth and the water in the centre is soft. A tripod was used so the rocks are sharp.

Image 2 – Sunset at Porth Nanven

NEUTRAL DENSITY FILTERS

Neutral Density filters, which range from pale grey to almost black, increase your exposure times by reducing the amount of light reaching the camera's sensor. They can be used in daytime to give an exposure value of a few seconds or, when it is darker, to give an exposure time, sometimes, in minutes rather than seconds. The longer shutter speeds enable you to achieve your desired effect, such as capturing movement or even making moving objects invisible.

The density of the filters varies from 1 stop up to 10 stops (and now even higher than this). There are different ways of describing the same density filter as, unfortunately, manufacturers do not use a standardised classification system to describe the strength of their filters.

F Stop Reduction (EV)	Optical Density (EV)	ND Factor
1	0.3	2
2	0.6	4
3	0.9	8
4	1.2	16
5	1.5	32
6	1.8	64
7	2.1	128
8	2.4	256
9	2.7	512
10	3.0	1024

Each column is a unit of measurement to describe how much light a particular filter will cut out. The f stops are shown in column 1 and for each stop of light reduction, this corresponds with a halving of light (i.e. the ND Factor: ½, ¼ and so on). The Optical Density is the log of the factor by which light is decreased. From the table you will see the corresponding classification, so that if you are using a 1.5 filter it will reduce your shutter speed by 5 exposure value (EV) stops and so on.

You can combine filters to give longer exposure times, but only do this when absolutely necessary, as the more optical accessories you place on your lens, the more image quality will be reduced. As the shutter speeds are slowed, a tripod becomes essential, unless you want movement in your image such as with ICM (Intentional camera movement).

Remote Release – These are advisable so that you do not have to touch the camera to press the shutter, which can cause a little movement in your shots. They are also essential if you are using the camera's Bulb function, which allows longer exposures than your camera's normal settings.

If you are using up to a 6 stop ND filter, you should be able to see through the viewfinder and so the autofocus will still work. If a higher density filter is being used, such as a 10 stop, then you cannot see anything through the viewfinder as it is almost black, so you will have to focus before putting on the filter, or manually focus.

To use the autofocus, while using a high density filter, the process is:

1. Using a tripod and with a remote attached to your camera, compose your image. Press the shutter half way down to focus and take an exposure reading without the filter on the lens.
2. Keeping your finger on the shutter, turn to Bulb Mode. The focus will then be set.
3. You are then able to take your hands off the camera and put on the filter.
4. On the Bulb Mode, you then control the length of time for your exposure.

The table shows the times for any given shutter speed and the effect of the different F-stop ND filters. Exposure times in seconds unless stated otherwise.

Exposure without Filters	3-Stop ND Filter)	6-Stop ND Filter	10-Stop ND Filter
1/500	1/60	1/8	2
1/250	1/30	1/4	4
1/125	1/15	1/2	8
1/60	1/8	1	15
1/30	1/4	2	30
1/15	1/2	4	1 min
1/8	1	8	2 mins
1/4	2	15	4 mins
1/2	4	30	8 mins
1	8	1 min	15 mins
2	15	2 mins	30 mins
4	30	4 mins	60 Mins
8	1 min	8 mins	2 hours
15	1.5 mins	15 mins	4 hours
30	2 mins	30 mins	8 hours

To use the chart, find the shutter speed given by your camera, without the ND filter in place, in the left hand column. Read across until you find the ND filter that you are using. This then gives the exposure length required. Alternatively, if you want a certain shutter speed for a specific effect, look across and then up at the top to find the ND filter that is required.

There are now lots of Apps available for your smartphone or tablet that will calculate the correct exposure time such as ND Timer, ND Calc, ND Exposure, Long Exposure Calculator, Quicosoft's Exposure Calculator and others. These Apps will firstly tell you the shutter speed required before you put on your ND filter. Once the filter is attached, they will tell you how many stops it is and so instantly tells you how long the shutter speed needs to be. They also have a built-in timer counting down the seconds, and some with alarms.

Whether you are using a chart or an App, they will give a general idea but over time you will get to know roughly how long you need in given conditions to achieve the results you want. You should bear in mind that as the shutter speeds become longer, the timing is less critical. Another point to remember when doing long exposure work is that the light can change during an exposure, which would affect your timing.

CAPTURING MOVEMENT OF THE SEA

Recording the movement of the sea in your images can be very effective and add a dreamy dimension to your photographs. Different effects can be achieved depending upon the speed and power of the incoming waves, and the shutter speed used to take the image. A shutter speed of 1 second upwards will produce a good effect, but don't be afraid to experiment with exposures that are much longer than this – several minutes if necessary.

The effect obtained depends on the lighting conditions at the time, the speed of the water and what shutter speed, and the shutter speed, in turn, is dependent on what filters are used, and the ISO and aperture settings chosen. We'll look through some examples to see the differences achievable.

Image 3 – Pier and Groynes

In image 3, the shutter speed was about 1 second and you can see the waves have been softened and lines are starting to appear in the movement of the water in the foreground.

In image 4, again the shutter speed was about 1 second and the waves have been softened once again. Here you can see the movement of the receding waves as lines in the foreground.

Image 4 – Receding Waves

In Image 5, the shutter speed was 1.3 seconds. The shutter was pressed as the sea started rushing towards the shore and the lines in the water appear to add detail to the composition.

Image 5 – Bantham

In image 6, a 10 stop neutral density filter has been used and the shutter speed was over 4 minutes. When using a shutter speed of this length, all detail has gone from the water and in your composition you are left with the structures in the scene. You need to think about what your composition will be like without the movement of the water to assist your composition, such as the railings leading the viewer in from the corner in this image and making an 'S' and so on. These types of images can be quite minimalist and work very well in black and white, as in image 7.

Image 6 – High Water at the Sea Pool

Image 7 – Boating Pool at Sunrise

If you want to capture the movement of the water coming towards a rock and flowing around it, then you need to work out how long this action takes, then adjust your shutter speed accordingly. Press the shutter when the sea starts to come towards the rock and this will result in lines around the rocks showing this movement. The image below shows movement around the rock and also some lace like effect in the foreground, which is quite attractive.

Image 8 – Rocks on the Beach

CAPTURING OTHER MOVEMENT

Long exposures can be used to capture any movement in the landscape not just waves and flowing water in rivers, but movement of grasses and leaves as well to give an impressionist feel to your image.

In image 9, with a shutter speed of 2 seconds a tripod was used and the grasses and the sea in the background can be seen moving while the sand in the foreground is quite sharp.

Long exposures can also be used to capture the movement of people and vehicles. In image 10 you can see a chap standing still looking at his phone while people and a bus are moving around him. He is sharp and the movement around him emphasises the action taking place.

In image 11 of the Gherkin in the City of London, the buildings and the bicycle are sharp, but movement is shown with the bus and person walking past.

Image 9 – Grasses at Seilebost

Image 10 – Time for texting

Image 11 – The Gherkin

If you want to show movement in your images, however, you need to ensure you get the shutter speed right. Too long and the sense of movement you are trying to show will be lost. In fact, moving objects may disappear altogether as with the detail of the sea in images with shutter speeds of minutes. With image 12, which had a shutter speed of only 0.3 seconds, the girl walking past has almost vanished, with only parts of her leg and feet visible.

There will obviously be times when this can be used to your advantage if you do not want people or moving objects in your photograph – have a shutter speed long enough so that they do not register at all.

Image 12 – Walking too fast

The image below had a shutter speed of well over 2 minutes and yet the people are still visible. In this case they were milling around on the slipway watching the sunset and consequently they appear as ghosts. This can obviously be used creatively as in this image, 'Graveyard of the Pier'.

Image 13 – Graveyard of the Pier

Long shutter speeds can be used to capture any sense of movement and can be particularly effective with **traffic trails** and **fireworks**.

Image 14 shows the traffic in both directions driving along the Embankment in London, with the rear red lights and the white front lights shown as continuous lines.

Image 15 shows fireworks going off outside the Chateau at Duras in SW France. The chateau is lit up and the fireworks are in the foreground.

Image 14 – Traffic trails

EQUIPMENT REQUIRED FOR LONG EXPOSURE PHOTOGRAPHY

- A sturdy tripod
- Neutral Density Filters
- Remote Release

Image 15 – Fireworks

INTENTIONAL CAMERA MOVEMENT (ICM)

Intentional camera movement is another technique that you can try to create some beautiful, impressionist and ethereal images. As in capturing movement with long exposure photography, ICM requires a slow shutter speed to introduce blur into the image. The difference being that with the previous examples, a tripod is used so that the part of the image that is not moving is sharp, whereas with ICM, a tripod is not used and the camera is deliberately moved so that everything in the image is blurred for a creative or artistic effect. The details are suppressed, giving an impressionistic feel to the scene.

There are many ways to use ICM to capture creative and unusual images. Just experiment and look at the results on your LCD screen to see how well your technique is working and be prepared to discard those that are not. This is the advantage of digital photography. The results are difficult to predict but the possibilities are limitless. There are no rules and it is fun to have a go!

The camera is usually handheld and works best with shutter speeds of between ¼ second and 5 seconds, depending on the effect you are trying to achieve. With this type of photography, the best effect is achieved with a simple, uncluttered scene, as it will still be recognizable even when blurred.

The images below have been taken with just a little movement to give an impressionist feel of the colours of autumn.

Image 16 – Impressionist Autumn Leaves

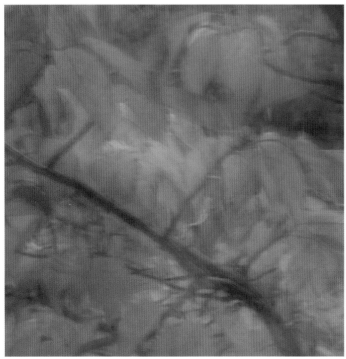

Image 17 – Autumn Leaves

The images can be panned, moving the camera from one side to the other (horizontally) or up and down (vertically) in more or less a straight line and these generally work best for different types of landscape. As you can see in image 18, landscapes and seascapes are best panned sideways following the horizon, but trees in image 19 show they are best panned in a vertical direction. The yachts in image 20 also lend themselves to a slight panning vertically, in this image for 0.3 seconds.

Image 18 – Panning Seascape

Image 19 – ICM Trees

Image 20 – Impressionist Yachts

Another form of panning is to track the movement so the subject is in sharper focus than the background. This is best achieved by starting to pan with the subject before the shutter is pressed. A couple of examples of this are shown. In Image 21 the London taxi is quite sharp whereas the background has streaks giving the movement. The same goes for the cyclist in Image 22.

Image 21 - Panning Taxi

Image 22 - Panning Cyclist

The other type of movement is completely random and, therefore, trial and error. The camera can be rotated, jiggled or any other movement. Try a shutter speed of about 4 seconds and experiment.

In the triptych below, instead of panning down which would reduce the flowers to streaks, the camera was held in one position and quickly moved to another for a shorter period, giving a shadow effect.

Image 23 – Blue flowers triptych

Other ideas for you to try:
Zooming out from the centre of the flowers was done with the two images below

Image 24 – Daisy Zooming

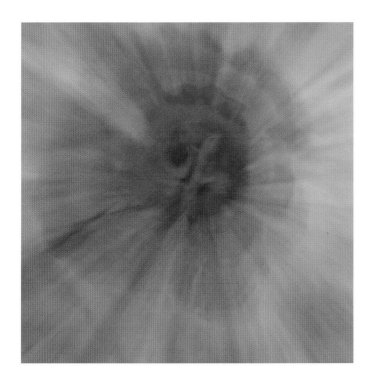

Image 25 – Red Roses Zooming out

Rotating the camera 360 degrees, which works well looking up at the tops of trees

Image 26 – Tree Rotating

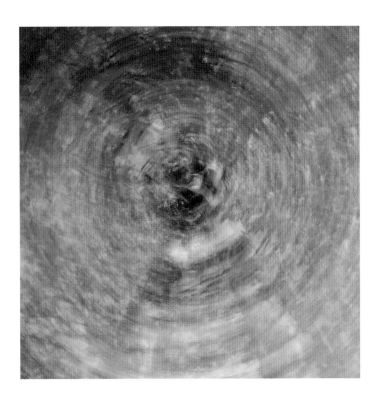

Image 27 – Tree Rotating 360 degrees

Circular motion to make more of an abstract image, as is done with the white rose images below:

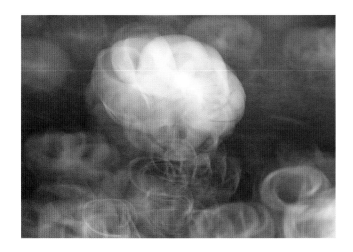

Images 28-30 – Roses in Circles

Intentional Camera Movement (ICM) requires a lot of trial and error, so keep taking images and see what the best types of movement and exposure times are for your subject. **Remember to keep the scene simple so that it is still recognizable even when blurred.**

MULTIPLE EXPOSURES

In photography a Multiple Exposure is when two or more exposures are blended or superimposed over each other to create a single image. The resulting photographic image shows the images layered over one another. This technique allows you to experiment with your shots and create surreal, unique and fascinating images. Essentially the images are merged or blended together into one image. They can be created in the dark room by stacking negatives, with a DSLR camera by using the Multiple Exposure function in the menu, or by blending the images together in Photoshop. In this section, however, we shall be dealing with multiple exposures taken in-camera. Multiple exposures (or composite images) in Photoshop will be dealt with later in the book.

With early film cameras, Multiple Exposures probably came about as the result of mistakes (as is often the case with something new). It was then possible to take a second image on top of the first when the photographer had forgotten to move the film on. Recently, however, intentional double exposures have become popular again as a way of creating unique images. Not all DSLRS have the Multiple Exposure function, but the list is growing all the time. Some now offer this capability with sophisticated blending modes to extend further the creative possibilities. Many smart phones also have Apps, such as 'Multiple Exposure for the iphone' and 'Photo Blender for Androids'.

At a basic level, in order to have more control of multiple exposure images, it is helpful to understand negative and positive values. White in photography is where the data has been burned out and there is no data to be brought back, nor are you able to overlay over it. Black, on the other hand, represents the unexposed areas and the second exposure will fill these parts of the image.

To demonstrate this, the first image is a silhouette of a sculpture taken against a white background, and the second an image looking up at branches with the blue sky in the background. In the resulting composite image you can see the branches and the blue sky appear in the very dark part of the image, but nothing at all shows in the white area.

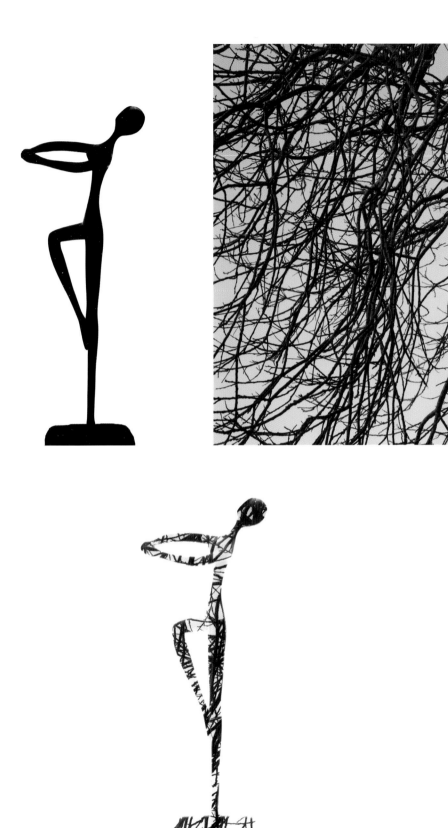

Images 31-33 – Silhouette

If, however, the first image is not completely black and white but toned, then parts of this image will come through rather than just the second image being seen in the silhouette, as shown in this series of shots. You can see the face of the child showing through the trees in the final composite image. The first image shows detail of the child and the sky is not completely white, so a hint of the second image shows through here as well, especially as the tree is very dark.

Images 34-36 – Arlo and Tree

Once you start adding more exposures, the process becomes very complicated. The best approach when starting out with Multiple Exposures is not to get too worried by the technical aspects, but to experiment and gain understanding from experience and trial and error. Some cameras take up to 10 shots and it can be as easy or as complicated as you like. The different layers of images can be taken using different lenses or a change of focus and can be positioned using Live View, if your camera has this function.

Cameras vary in their settings, so you will have to look at your camera's manual to see what functions are available to you. To give you an idea of the type of settings to look for, Canon DSLRs, for example, have Average, Additive, Light and Dark blending modes for the merging of the separate exposures.

Additive – similar to the way film records light, the resulting image gradually becomes lighter and lighter and you will need to compensate by underexposing a little.

Average – compensates for the light and gives an average blend.

Bright – is meant for night shots, and only the bright areas of the images are registered.

Dark – The darker parts of the image are combined and the lighter areas are suppressed.

With Nikon DSLRs, Auto works out the exposure calculations for you (like Average above); with Auto off, this is then the same as Additive, and you will need to work out exposure yourself or use it creatively.

Canon cameras with the Multiple Exposure function allow you to combine an image already taken on the memory card in the normal way with another image taken in the multiple exposure mode. This means the resultant multiple exposure does not have to be two consecutive images. This enables you to have more attempts at getting the image right. For example, you might have the silhouette you want, but would like to try different textures or scenes to see which works best.

Nikon allows you to select any two images on the memory card and combine using 'Image Overlay' which, in effect, gives you even more control over your exposures.

The multiple exposure setting is usually disabled by default, which means it has to be activated.
As can be seen, it is essential to look at your camera's manual to see what settings are available to you. We'll now go through some ideas that you can try. If you want to add texture to an image, take the texture layer first, then the subject. This can be seen in the image of the vase and flower.

Image 37 – Vase with flower

To create an image with an impressionistic feel, take several exposures of the same subject, some being slightly out of focus as was done with the tree opposite, which has 5 exposures. This method works better if there are not too many elements in the scene.

Image 38 - Pink Blossom ME

The same goes for the cobbled street with people walking towards the archway. The simplicity of the scene means the viewer can still see what is going on but the feel is impressionist.

Image 39 - Chateau at Narbonne

The railway station images also work because the lines leading in the viewer help to simplify the rather complex scenes.

Image 40 - At the Station

Image 41 - Hustle and Bustle at the Station

Abstract shots may be taken combining whatever takes your fancy and some will work, and some will not! As mentioned with the ICM technique, just experiment and see what you come up with. Remember you can change lens in between exposures, or change the focus. Having one shot sharp and one with a soft focus can work well.

These shots were taken of a small planter to create soft abstract images, the first with 2 and the other with 3 exposures.

Image 42 – Blue Planter

Image 43 - Blue Planter 2

The image below was combined from two exposures of flowers with one being out of focus, and positioned using Live View on the back of the camera.

Image 44 – White Flowers

REMEMBER

Set your camera to Multiple Exposure mode.
Shoot your first layer (or select one from your camera's memory card, if possible).
Then shoot the second and subsequent layers. Use Live View, if you have it, to position the shots.
Keep images simple – subtlety and simplicity is the key when combining images.
There are no rules to shooting multiple exposures so be as experimental as you like.

USING DIFFERENT LENSES

Another way to rekindle your motivation and creativity is to play with a different lens, some of which can give pleasing and unexpected results.

MACRO LENS

Whole books have been written on macro photography, and if you want to specialise in this field you will need to learn the technical aspects first. However, don't be intimidated, have a go and see what you come up with. You might be surprised with your innovative images if you just let your creativity take over.

Experiment with change in depth of field and different points of focus to enable you to come up with some creative, more unusual images. A small aperture (high number) is often required to produce sharpness across a three-dimensional subject, to get all or most of the main subject in focus. When magnifying a subject, you also magnify movements caused by camera shake. A tripod and remote release are therefore usually required. If you are photographing a subject that cannot be arranged roughly on the same plane, you will have to decide which parts of it you want in focus. Experiment with wider (smaller number) apertures which will throw more of the subject out of focus and may produce pleasing artistic effects.

Image 45 - Agapanthus

Image 46 - Fading Rose Macro

After the rain can be an excellent time to search for macro subjects in the garden when everything is dripping with droplets of rain water, as shown in the image of the rose and the grasses.

Image 47 - Raindrops on the Rose

Image 48 - Grass with raindrops

A macro lens has more uses than just for extreme close-up work, as can be seen in these images of the backlit blossom including branches in the background, which adds to the composition. They are very soft and delicately frame the blossom itself. This can be extended to include even more of the scene to give gentle, painterly backgrounds.

Image 49 – Blacklit Blossom Triptych

LENSBABY LENSES

If you really want to have fun and try something unique and totally different, then experiment with a Lensbaby.

Lensbaby is a company that makes a range of quirky selective focus lenses that are worth looking into. Its lenses are designed for fun and give creative dreamy, ethereal, glowing soft focus effects. There is a learning curve when using them, and the more you practise and explore, the better you get. In the range is the Lensbaby Twist that has a twisty, swirly blur and the Lensbaby Spark, which allows you to move the lens around to change the 'sweet spot' as well as the blurred area which surrounds it. It is beautifully atmospheric and unique and works well with portraiture to give an ethereal look. The Lensbaby Velvet 56 is a very popular lens with selective focusing and creamy bokeh effects.

Lensbabies are manual lenses and the focus is done manually. They are for use in selective focus photography and to create bokeh effects. At large apertures, the lenses produce soft, glowing images, whereas at small apertures, the images are sharp and yet subtly unique.

Images 50-52 were taken with a Lensbaby Velvet 56 and you can see the soft focus glow, which is so appealing.

Image 50 – Fading Beauty with Lensbaby

Image 51 - Roses Lensbaby

Image 52 - Cowslip

Vintage Russian Lenses can also be used for soft focus, bokeh effects. They can be inexpensive and may be picked up on e-Bay. Created in the USSR between 1950 and 1980, the Jupiter range, such as the Jupiter 9 85mm f2, and Jupiter 11 135 mm f/4, are worth tracking down. Zenit and Helios lenses are also worth looking out for.

A **Fish Eye Lens** can also be great to play with. It is a super wide-angle lens which distorts the image but it can be used creatively.

Using Depth of Field
You do not even need to change lens to get the bokeh effect. The image of the ferns below was taken at 92mm, using a Canon 24-105 mm lens, with a very shallow depth of field of f/4, looking into the low sun to create this backlit effect. Care must be taken not to include the sun in the image, unless that is the effect you are experimenting with.

Image 53

OTHER CREATIVE IDEAS

There is potential for creative images all around us if we allow ourselves to see them. Sometimes it takes time to look away from the obvious and find something more unusual. Try looking at reflections in windows and in water, at patterns on rust, rocks and in ice, and even abstract images and landscapes in damp mould. You might be surprised at what you can find – just let your imagination wander.

Just to give you a few examples, the two images opposite are reflections of St Paul's Cathedral in the windows of nearby buildings. Glimpses of the interior of the buildings adds to the mystique.

Images 54-55 – Reflections of St Pauls

The image below of lavender seen through a glass gives a distorted impressionist, abstract feel.

Image 56 - Lavender through glass

Rust patterns are always fun. The patterns in this rusting wheelbarrow could appear to be landscapes taken from the air.

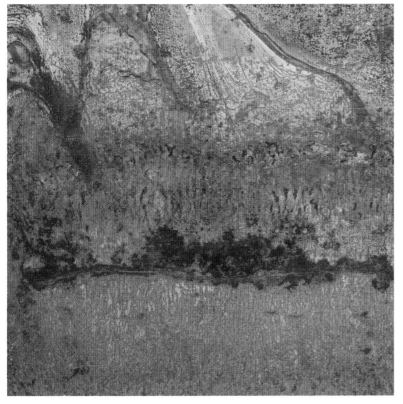

Images 57-58 - Rust Abstract

The mould on the wall of an old building resemble trees. It was raining hard outside and the drips of water rolling down the interior wall of the chateau, give the impression of tree trunks.

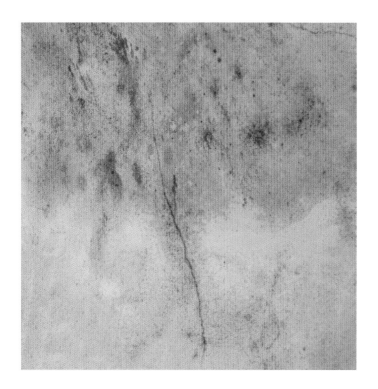

Images 59-60 – Trees in the Mould

The images below are reflections of trees in a shallow stream, which give a painterly feel. As you can see from the examples, **images are everywhere – you just need to look around more closely.**

'Vision is the art of seeing what is invisible to others.'

Jonathan Swift

Images 61-62 – Tree Reflection

USING PHOTOSHOP FOR CREATIVE PHOTOGRAPHY

Photoshop has been around for over 25 years now and is a highly successful editing tool for the creative industry. So successful that the word has become a verb – we all talk about Photoshopping our images and everyone knows exactly what we mean.

Many photographers use Photoshop to enhance a shot by minor tweaking with flexible non destructive editing tools. But it can also be harnessed to create beautiful composite images. The only limit to the creative process is the photographer's imagination but experimentation can lead to a place beyond that. Composite images can evolve and take on a life of their own. You might not be impressed by what you have created but, on the other hand, you might see possibilities in an aspect of a technique and follow through on it to produce something original.

In this section we will go through the most important techniques in the making of such composite images, i.e. layers and layer masks, which are essential for non-destructive editing. Who knows, you may achieve something beyond your wildest dreams.

Image 63 – Original Penguins

The starting shot of the composite image below was that of these penguins in image 63, found in some street art in the Brick Lane area of London. The next stage was to place the starting image on a snowy scene of Dartmoor as in Image 64. Texture layers were then added to blend the whole together as can be seen in the final image No 65. This composite image was achieved using the techniques explained in the following pages.

Image 64 – 2nd stage Penguins

Image 65 – Final Penguins

USING LAYERS

We start off looking at layers which are essential for non-destructive editing. But, most importantly, if you have saved your image with the layers in place, you can go back and change your document at any time.

A layer is one image stacked on top of another. Below we create some layers on a new blank document to help you understand the process.

Go to File and click on New to create a new document. Then using one of the selection tools at the top of the left hand panel, create a shape on the new document and then click on:

Layer > New Fill Layer > Solid Colour > OK. Then select a colour.

You will then see the shape in the colour selected in your new document. You will also see this colour and shape in the layers palette on the right hand side as a new layer on top of the white background. Do this several times with different shapes and colours, building up your layers. With the example here, you can see in the layers palette that the blue layer is on top, then the yellow, then the red, and at the bottom, the green layer.

Screenshot 1

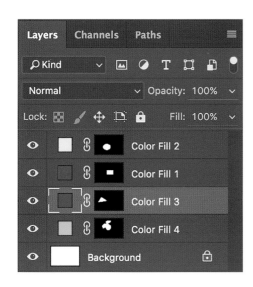

When working on a particular layer, the layer must be highlighted. If you want to change the order then highlight the layer, and click and drag to its new position.

You can see from the layers palette that the blue layer is now below the red and yellow layers.

Screenshot 2

You can hide a layer by clicking on the eye icon on the left hand side. If you want to change the opacity of a layer, then highlight the layer and change the opacity slider at the top of the layers palette. These changes can now be seen on the screen below. You will see the eye icon on the red layer is now removed and the opacity of the yellow layer has been changed from 100% to 55%.

To take this further so that you can build up composite images and to give you complete control over your final image, you will need to understand Layer Masks. Each image is added as a separate layer, and you will be able to select which parts of each image you want to show through. We now work through this process and your understanding will greatly increase as you go through the different sections as layer masks are used every time.

Screenshot 3

69

USING A LAYER MASK

The use of a layer mask is essential for composite images to give a seamless blending of two or more images. When images on various layers are required to be part of the overall composite image, it is possible to use the Eraser tool to rub out unwanted areas until the image looks correct. However, the problem with this method is that if you make a mistake you cannot easily 'undo', apart from going back through the History. You are not able to change your mind later and go back.

ADDING A LAYER MASK

Open your background image.
Then open the image you want to add to the background.
Show both images on the screen and click and drag the 2nd image on to the background.
(Alternatively you can select, copy and paste)

Use the Move tool to position the new image. Some transformation maybe required:
Edit > Transform > Scale
(Make sure the upper layer is highlighted)
Add **Layer Mask** to this top layer – this may be created by

1. Clicking on the Layer Mask icon (white circle within a grey square) at the bottom of the Layers palette, or

2. Via Layer > Add Layer Mask > Reveal All

The layer will now have two rectangles – one is the image thumbnail and one for the layer mask. The link between the two ensures that the image and its mask are locked together so that if the image is moved, the mask will move with it.

If you want to work on the image itself, then ensure the image rectangle of the active layer is on (i.e. has the white outline around it). If you want to work on the layer mask, ensure the layer mask icon is on.

We are now going to work through the above by adding a bolt on to a door.

Both images are now open in Screenshot 4 and the bolt has been dragged on to the background image in Screenshot 5 using the Move tool. You will see in the Layers Palette on the right, that the bolt is now a different layer above the background door image.

Screenshot 4

Screenshot 5

The lock is obviously too large for the door so we have to scale the image to look correct and then we are in a position to start using our layer mask so that we are left with just the bolt and not the rest of the image.

Screenshot 6

You will see in the above screenshot that the bolt is now the correct size and a layer mask has been added. This is the rectangle to the right of the image thumbnail. With this layer mask highlighted, we can now use our brush to remove the part of this image not wanted, zooming in close to make this easier and changing from black to white when a mistake has been made. (Full instructions on page 74).

Screenshot 7

You can now see this done in screenshot 7, but you will notice that as the image was large in comparison with the background image, it appears too sharp and needs softening. This is easily remedied; with the image thumbnail highlighted, click on Filter > Blur > Gaussian Blur (as shown below). You will also notice that the part of the bolt image that has been hidden shows on the layer mask icon in black.

Screenshot 8

WORKING ON A LAYER MASK

The foreground and background colours should be black and white respectively.
Choose a suitable brush (Ctrl B) – select brush size (brackets up and down) and choose softness/hardness (in Tool bar).

With brush opacity at 100% and foreground colour on black, the brush reveals the layer beneath.

To restore an area, change the foreground colour to white (Shortcut 'x'). The brush then paints the image back in again.

You can change between black and white foreground colours with different opacities/pressures and brush sizes to create the image you want.

If you forget to click on the rectangle containing the layer mask, you will paint black (or white) on your image. To undo – Ctrl Z or go back in the History.

When working on the edges of the imported image, zoom right in (Ctrl +).

If you have reduced the size of the imported image, you may find it is too sharp, in which case highlight the image icon (left hand rectangle) go to Filter > Blur > Gaussian Blur and add just a little (maybe 0.6 pixels). You can also make adjustments to this layer by again highlighting the left hand rectangle and going to Image > Adjustments > Levels etc.

(If you are using a Mac computer – replace Ctrl with CMD (Command) and Alt with Option keys). A full list of the most commonly used shortcuts may be found at the back of the book.

Duplicating/Moving a Layer Mask – If you want the same mask to appear on a different layer then hold Alt, click on the layer mask and drag into the new layer. You can still change this layer mask if required on part of the image.

If you want to remove the mask and put on another layer, then don't hold the Alt key, just click and drag the mask to the layer where you want it.

Adjustment Layers, for example Hue & Saturation or Levels, already have a layer mask. So after the adjustments have been made, these can be applied only to the areas you select by brushing out on the layer mask where you do not want the adjustments to be made.

We are now going to look at how we can apply layers and layer masks to your photographs and to give you ideas for making creative composite images. They can be as complicated as you want with dozens of layers if necessary, but mastering the techniques and letting your imagination flow need not be so complicated. Just a couple of images blended together can create wonderful effects. We are going to start by adding texture to an image as in the one here of the fish. A photo was taken of the fish on a plate and an image of a wave was added to the top. The final composite image on the next page was created by changing the opacity and hiding the parts of the wave layer that were not wanted using the layer mask. We will go into full details in the next section.

Image 66 – Fish on a plate

Image 67 – The sea texture

Image 68 – Fish on a plate – Final image

ADDING A TEXTURE LAYER

Adding a texture layer or overlay can enhance your images by adding depth and can be an effective creative tool, whether by giving the image a dreamy, painterly effect or a timeless, emotional quality.

By adding a textured image such as that of rocks, peeling paint, or net curtains, depending on the subject matter, a textured effect can be achieved on your original image. Texture layers do not suit all images, but can work well with certain subject matter, such as flowers, landscapes and old buildings.

Free textures may be found on-line, but to be completely original it is best to start your own texture file. Whenever you see a great texture, take a photo and put it in this file, then when you need an overlay for an image, you will have plenty to choose from.

We are now going to go through adding a texture layer by opening both a background image and a texture overlay in Photoshop. On the left you will see a girl walking past the clock shop and on the right a rough stone texture.

Screenshot 9

With the texture image highlighted, use the Move tool and click and drag this texture on top of the background. You will see in the Layers Palette that the texture now appears as a layer above the background layer. The texture image can now be closed.

The texture layer can be moved to the required position and the opacity changed to reveal the background through the texture. In the screenshot below you will see the Opacity in the Layer Palette has been reduced to 39% and you can see the texture on the image.

Screenshot 10

If you are happy with your image to have the texture evenly over the background, then the image is now finished. If, however, you would like to reveal parts of the background more, then you will need to add a layer mask. With the texture layer highlighted, click on the layer mask icon on the bottom of the layers palette and the layer mask rectangle will appear. You are then able to use your brush and bring through the parts of the image you would like to have less texture.

Remember to change the opacity of the brush or you will have 100% of the background coming through and this will not look right. It is easier to start with a low percentage and gradually build up to get the image you want. Here you can see the windows and the girl have been partially revealed by using the layer mask, using the brush on opacity 6%. The clocks were also brought through even more to draw attention to them. When working on this type of image, remember to be subtle around the edges of your subject. Below is the finished image.

Screenshot 11

REMEMBER

Keep your own file of texture images – eg raindrops, peeling paint, rocks, net curtains etc.
Be subtle around the edges when using a layer mask and build up gradually.

To show how different images can look when using different texture layers, look at these examples. Using the same original photo below, the first image opposite has had a raindrop layer added as well as a layer using the colour range technique shown on page 86. On the second, a rough rock texture layer was added and the image was then converted to black and white, and sepia toned.

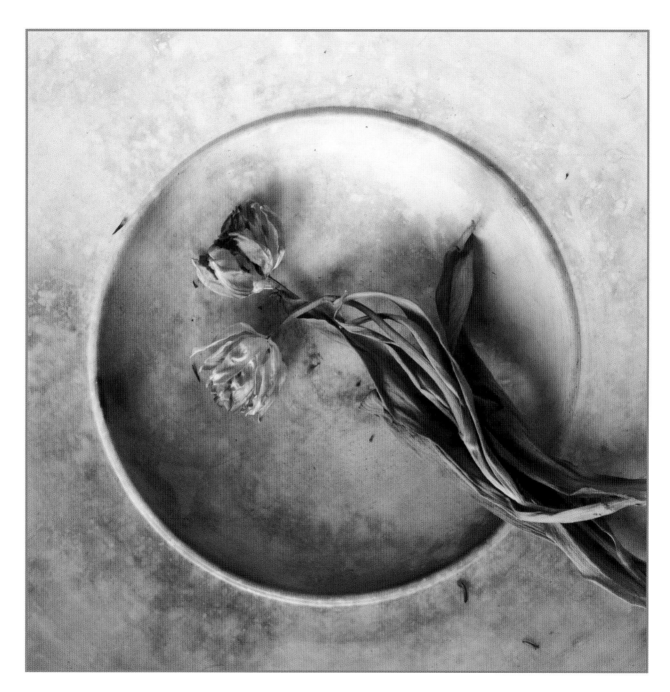

Image 69 – Two Tulips Original

Image 70 – Two Tulips

Image 71 – Two Tulips Mono

In the image of the field of sunflowers below, the same technique with a rough rock texture overlay was used and then the image was converted to black and white and sepia toned. The original image had a blue sky and fluffy white clouds and this treatment has completely transformed it. A dark vignette was also used to darken the outside area and draw the viewer into the centre of the image. How to achieve a vignette is explained opposite.

Image 72 – Field of sunflowers

This method can be used to combine any two or more layers together. You could try adding sheet music, raindrops and so on. Try and see what works. Text has been used as the overlay for the historic scene taken at Bristol Harbour below.

Image 73 – Graffiti door

VIGNETTING

In order to draw the viewer into your image, sometimes it helps to add a dark or light vignette around the edges. To do this use the Lasso tool to select the area you want to be affected and feather the edges by 100 pixels (tool bar). Go to Select and click on Inverse so the area outside your selection will be chosen. Add a Levels Adjustment Layer and use the slider for the effect you want, **remembering to be subtle**.

LAYER BLENDING MODES

The blending modes give us a range of alternative ways for a layer to interact with, or 'blend' with, the layer or layers below it. Without layer blending modes, the only way we have of blending layers together is by reducing the opacity of a layer. By default, the blending modes are set at Normal. This means the texture layer is opaque, so that nothing can be seen beneath it until the opacity of the layer has been reduced. You may prefer to make this texture partially transparent by selecting another blending mode. So even with the opacity set to 100%, the layer below still shows through.

To scroll through the blending modes, found at the top of the Layers Palette, to see the effect for yourself: highlight a blending mode and use the arrows up and down or scroll with the mouse.

The blending modes are arranged in different groupings: Darken, Lighten, Contrast, Comparative and Composite modes. The most commonly used are: Soft Light, Multiply, Screen and Overlay. This is a very technical topic and whole books have been written on just this subject. Photographers, however, do not need to go into too much detail – scrolling down the blending modes to see if any suit a particular type of image. Just experiment and see if something works. The opacity of the layer may also be changed to reduce the effect of the particular blending mode.

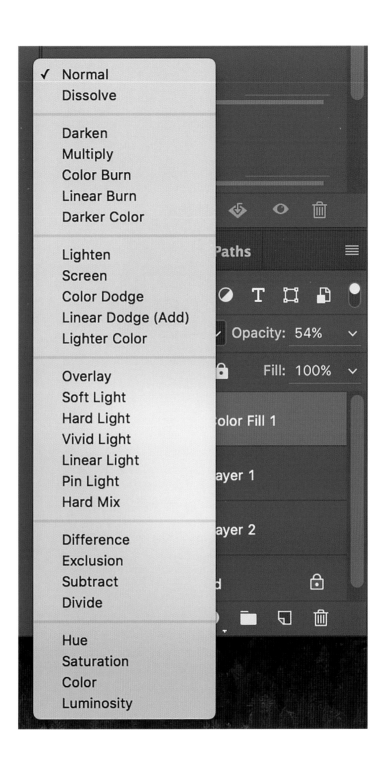

COLOUR RANGE

Sometimes you may take a photograph only to feel that the subject has no connection with its background; an object on a plate for example. If you want to make the image appear more as a whole, you can blend the image into its background. You could use a texture layer but another way of doing this is to use a section of the subject and blend it with the background. This has the effect of giving the whole image the same colour palette and also some texture from the subject, as can be seen in the image of the fig below.

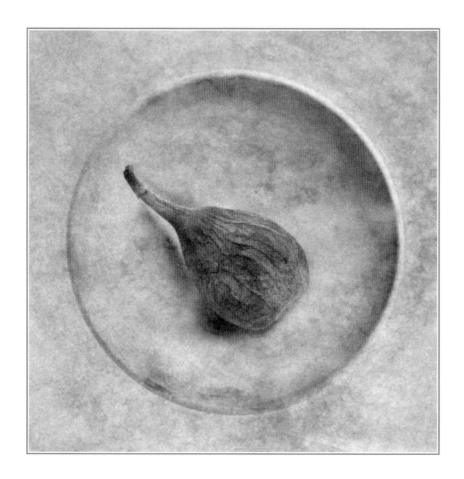

Image 74 - The Fig

To demonstrate this, we shall go through the process by which we achieve the final composite image of some drooping flowers in a vase.

You can see in screenshot 13 that a small rectangle selection has been made of the flower on the left. This selection is then copied and pasted by going to Edit > Copy > Paste.

 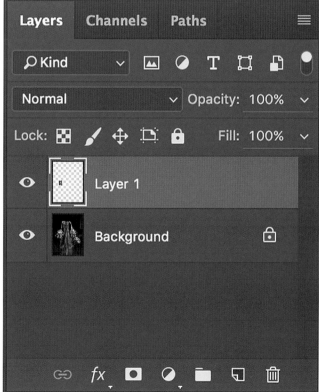

Screenshots 13 and 14

This small selection has now appeared as a new layer above the background layer in the layers palette (Screenshot 14).

Click on Edit > Transform > Scale (see below).

Then click on the corner and drag the selection over the whole image. As you can see in the screenshot opposite, the selection of the flower is covering the image of the vase and flowers. Change the opacity until you get the effect you are after, making sure this petal layer is highlighted. Here the Opacity is set at 42%.

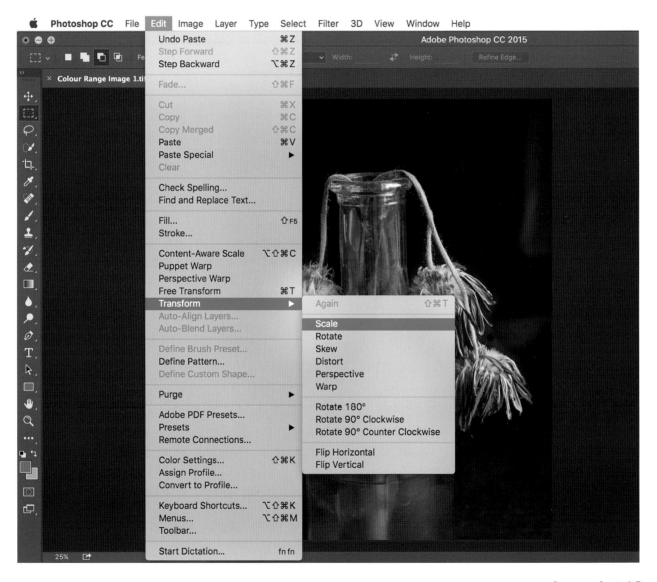

Screenshot 15

Add a layer mask and select the brush tool. Bring through as much of the flower underneath as you want. Most of the flowers have been brought through here with care being taken around the edges. They need to be soft, so a soft brush on a lower opacity is best. You can see in the Layer Mask, the rectangle to the right of the flower icon, the black circles where the flowers are showing through from the image below.

This process was done twice, by adding another selection of the flowers and scaling over the image, changing the opacity and then bringing the flowers through with a layer mask, until we achieve the desired result.

To finish off the image, we add a White Layer, and this process is explained in the next section.

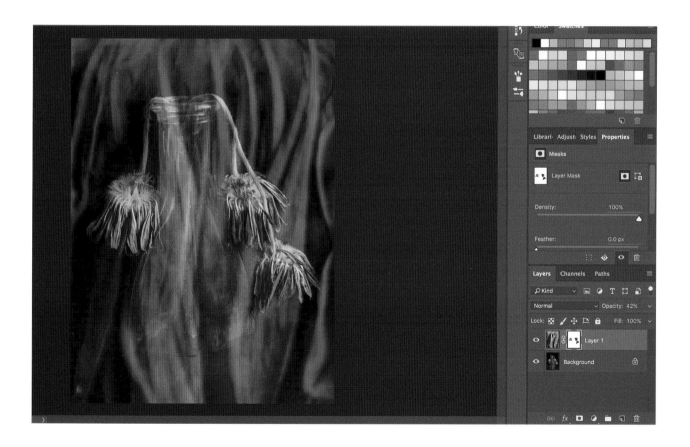

Screenshot 16

ADDING A WHITE LAYER (FOR A PASTEL EFFECT)

A good way to give an image a pastel effect is to add a white layer. We shall continue with the example in the Colour Range section. You add a White Layer by going to

Layer > New Fill Layer > Solid Colour

Click OK in the New Layer dialogue box. You will then be given a choice of colours in the Colour Picker chart. Click on the left hand top corner and press OK. You will now see your image has gone completely white and that a new layer has been added in the Layer Palette on the right hand side.

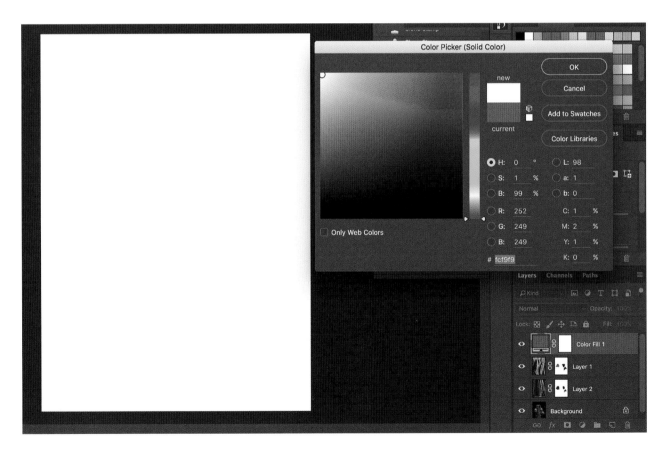

Screenshot 17

Making sure the blend mode is on Normal, change the opacity of this layer from 100% to about 40%, or whatever looks right to you. You can then click on the Layer Mask and, keeping the brush on a low opacity, gradually bring through the flowers and they will be revealed from the image below. In this case part of the vase was also brought through with a very low opacity brush.

Using the layer mask with this type of image, the edges of the subject can be kept very soft with the brush on a low opacity. It is not necessary to go precisely round the edges as you do not want the edges looking sharp.

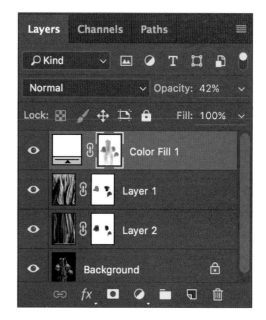

Screenshot 18

Finished image with colour range and white layers.

Image 75 – Drooping flowers

MERGING AND FLATTENING LAYERS

Merge Down – Merges (combines) the active layer with the layer immediately below.

Merge Visible – Merges all those layers that are visible, i.e. all that have the 'eye' icon on.

Flatten Image – Merges all layers into one layer

Stamp Visible (Shift+Ctrl+Alt+E) – Merges all the visible layers but the merged layer appears as a new extra layer at the top. On this composite layer you can sharpen, clone and edit in various ways without affecting the layers that contributed to the image up to this state. The Stamp Visible layer can be deleted or a layer mask can be added to this layer if you want to reveal parts of the lower layers. This also enables you to delete the layer and go back to your original layers if you want to change something at a later time.

ADDING SOFTNESS TO IMAGE

There are many ways to add softness to an image in Photoshop and we are going to go through four different processes: using the Clarity slider in the Raw file, the Gaussian Blur filter, the Orton Effect and finally the High Pass Filter.

Using the Clarity Slider – open the **RAW file** twice, first as a sharp image with the Clarity Slider in its normal position, then open again with the Clarity taken down to 0.

On the soft image – Select All, Copy and Paste on top of the sharp image.

(This method ensures the soft image is exactly positioned over the sharp image – if you click and drag from one image to the other, then you are positioning by eye)

Add a layer mask to the soft image and bring through what you would like sharp in the image. Remember to be subtle and keep the edges soft (i.e. change opacity of the brush – not keeping it on 100%).

CLARITY SLIDER

We shall go through this method using the image of the Seagull. Firstly, open the Raw file in Photoshop and then open it again with the Clarity at 0. The screenshot below shows the Clarity slider being taken down to 0 and the resulting very soft image.

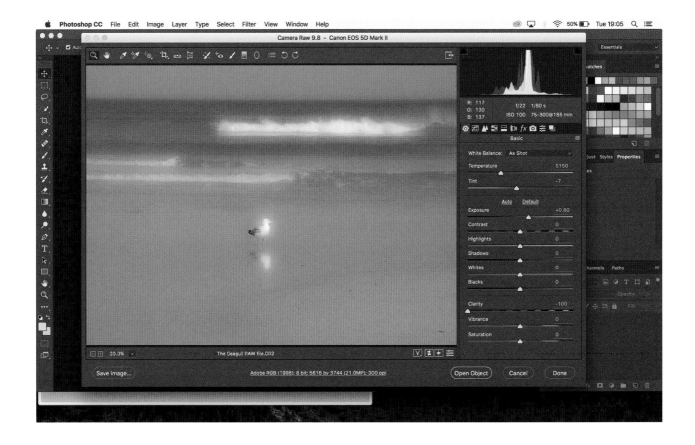

Screenshot 19

Open this soft image and copy and paste it on top of the sharp image already opened. You then need to apply a layer mask and, using your brush, bring through the seagull from the sharp layer. The seagull will then be sharp against the soft background, as can be seen in the image below. To finish this image, it was cropped into a square and finally a white layer added to give a soft pastel effect to the whole image. This method works extremely well with photos of the sea, although you could try it with any of your pictures to see the effect it creates.

Image 76 – The Seagull

GAUSSIAN BLUR

This method can be used when you need to soften an image and also when you do not have a Raw file.

Copy the background layer so that you have two identical layers one above the other (Ctrl J). On the top layer go to Filter > **Blur > Gaussian Blur** adding as much blur as you want. Then add a layer mask and, once again, bring through the part you want to be sharp. You could try changing the blending mode to Overlay or Soft Light; both are part of the Contrast group, but Soft Light is more subtle.

ORTON EFFECT

Similar to the technique above, the Orton effect uses Gaussian Blur, but the blending mode is changed to Multiply instead of Normal. This effect gives an image a soft focus with a glow. Choose a strong image that would benefit from a dreamy treatment. This effect gives a somewhat surreal image, slightly out of focus while retaining lots of edge detail.

Open your sharp image, lightened and slightly overexposed. Then copy this layer (Ctrl J). Add Gaussian Blur to the top layer. Change the blending mode to Multiply.

Use the Opacity slider to give the effect you want. You can still use a layer mask to leave parts of the image sharp if you prefer.

The 'before and after' effect can be seen in the images of the poppies. You can see the slightly dreamy soft effect of the image on the bottom.

Images 77-78 –Poppies

HIGH PASS FILTER

Another way to soften an image is to use the **High Pass Filter**. This creates a beautiful, ethereal soft focus effect.

Duplicate the background layer and then go to Filter > Other > High Pass. You can experiment with the radius – the higher the number, the softer the image. Go to Image > Adjustments > Invert to invert the layer and change the blending mode to Soft Light. Add a layer mask to bring through the parts of the image you want sharp, such as the eyes in a portrait.

This technique was used in the image opposite of the bluebells in the misty woods.

To use **High Pass Filter** for **sharpening**, do not invert and change the blending mode to Overlay.

Images 79-80 –Bluebells in the Misty Wood

REMEMBER

Always be subtle, especially round the edges of your masked subjects.

Saving your final image and keeping your layers open with layer masks means you can always go back at a later date if you change your mind.

Use the techniques and experiment to **create your own style**, allowing your passion in your photography to come across to the viewer.

USEFUL SHORTCUTS IN PHOTOSHOP

(For use with a **Mac computer** – replace Ctrl with CMD (Command) and Alt with Option keys)

Ctrl A = Select All

Ctrl C = Copy

Ctrl V = Paste

Ctrl P = Print

Ctrl Z = Undo (Repeat Ctrl Z for going back to original)

Ctrl Alt Z = Undo (Continuously going back in history)

Ctrl + = Zoom In

Ctrl – = Zoom Out

Ctrl B = Brush

[(left bracket) = smaller brush size

] (right bracket) = larger brush size

Ctrl J = Copy background layer

x – changes foreground colour (with mask from black to white or white to black)

Shift + Ctrl + Alt + E = Stamp Visible (merges all the visible layers, with the merged layer appearing at the top of the layer stack)

THE WAY AHEAD

Experimentation is the key to creativity, so try some of the techniques suggested both in-camera and using Photoshop and see what you come up with. Even try combining both by finalising an image in Photoshop after employing some of the other techniques. Explore the possibilities in your photography to create your own personal style, in which your own vision and emotion, and passion for your subject come across to the viewer.

Look at the work of not only photographers, but artists in other fields. You might get inspiration and ideas you can translate into your work.

But remember to have fun!

SOME PHOTOGRAPHERS' WEBSITES TO LOOK AT:

Valda Bailey – www.valdabailey.com
Doug Chinnery – www.dougchinnery.com
Chris Friel – www.cfriel.com
Irene Froy – www.irenefroy.co.uk
Glenys Garnett – www.ggcreativeimages.co.uk
Nicki Gwynn-Jones – www.nickigwynnjones.zenfolio.com
Michael Orton – www.michaelortonphotography.com

FOR TIPS AND IDEAS ON PHOTOSHOP TECHNIQUES:

www.adobetv.com – click on the Photoshop icon and you will find Tutorial videos for all levels.

Image 81 – Historique Aquitaine

HISTORIQUE AQUITAINE

Below are Linda's comments on her recent project 'Historique Aquitaine'.

'A project I worked on over the last couple of years was based on my love of the character of France. I really enjoyed the historic nature of the Aquitaine region where I was staying at the time. I became fascinated with the old buildings and started taking images of the details, including religious sculptures, gargoyles, balconies, windows, doors and door knockers. Indeed, anything that caught my attention as unusual whilst, at the same time, being typical of the region. I wanted to capture the texture in these images and for this I needed soft light, so they could be taken at any time on an overcast day, or even in the shade.

'I wanted to add something to the subject matter in order to look beyond the obvious and create my own personal interpretation. I decided I needed an overlay to combine with the subject matter in order to add the atmosphere I was trying to convey and put it into context. Eventually I came across some old worn books containing the weekly children's journal from the 1850s 'La Semaine des Enfants'. These journals contained many illustrations, some of which I photographed to use as the overlays. These images were put on top of the photo of the architectural subject matter in Photoshop with the opacity changed and, using a layer mask, I brought through what I wanted from the original subject.

'I really enjoyed working on this project and it certainly gave my photography focus while in France.

'The image on the next page shows the illustration on the opening page of all the journals and I combined this with a sculpture of a child, as I felt this suited the title page.'

Image 82 - Logo